CHOICES FOR *Life*

Presented to

_____

On this ____ *day of* _____

_____

By _____

_____

Personal Note

CHOICES FOR *Life*

THOMAS NELSON PUBLISHERS
Nashville

Contents

Introduction

*C*hoices, choices, choices.

It seems we are faced with so many of them each day. What should I have for lunch? Which car should I buy? Where should I go to school? Which movie should I rent?

Choices seem to be more complicated today than in days gone by. We have more to choose from today, and that can make choosing more difficult. Back when we only had three flavors of ice cream—chocolate, strawberry and vanilla—everyone had a favorite and choosing was easy. Suddenly, more than ten times as many flavors are available, and it can take longer to choose a flavor than to eat it! It's nice to have a choice, but choosing can be hard.

In days gone by, when a baby was conceived fewer choices were easily available compared to today. Choosing is harder now. Pressures and demands come from so many places. Parents, friends, spouses, employers, teachers, counselors and society itself all seem to want to have a voice in what you choose to do when you find out you're expecting a baby.

"I have set before you life and death, blessing and cursing; therefore choose life, that both you and your descendants may live" (Deuteronomy 30:19). God spoke these words to His people long ago, but they also apply to us. Today you have before you choices of much greater importance than ice cream flavors. As you face choices about your life and the life of the baby who is in your care, you can be strengthened by reading the words of others who have faced choices, choices for life.

Many of the authors whose writings are contained in

these pages have faced choices like those you are facing. Rick was a star football player when he and his girlfriend conceived their first child. Terry was a Christian college student when one evening of indiscretion resulted in her pregnancy. Stephanie was not a Christian, but since her abortion she has found peace with God. Each author has written from his or her own experience. They desire to share with you about the decisions they made and how their lives have been affected. You see, these really are choices for life because they will be with you for a lifetime. Through the choices you make you can grow as a person.

A few of the authors were not faced with pregnancies out of wedlock. Melinda's story reveals how she has chosen to love and to let herself be loved by a son born with Down's syndrome. Pam assists many women through the childbirth process and has come to understand powerful truths about spiritual birth as well.

Though I do not know you personally, I do know that God desires to give you the strength you need to carry out your choices for life. To help you gain the strength, Sandra Aldrich has written a thirty-one-day devotional series for you. After you've read the stories about choices my friends have made, begin Sandra's devotions. If you'll read one each day, you'll finish in just one short month. You'll find that God will be speaking to you in the secret places of your heart as you read. You may hear from Him in ways you have not in the past. You see, He has chosen to love you and to care deeply for you. He has all the strength you'll ever need. ❧

Harriet R.T. Lewis
General Editor
Falls Church, Virginia 1993

Reflections
of
Life

My Choice

by Teresa Eklund

Dearest One,

In your recent letter you asked about the decision behind your birth and open adoption. How do I begin to tell you about that time in our lives?

When I discovered your existence, my world came crashing down around me. I felt as if a weight had been put around my shoulders and I had been cast into the deepest sea. I was drowning. Please understand; it wasn't you. It was what I had done to conceive you.

You see, I was young, and your birth father and I were not married. I was supposed to be a God-fearing Christian. I read Scripture, I prayed and I went to church. To be an unwed mother was not part of the equation. But it had become a part of mine.

The decision of whether to abort you was never really an issue with me. It crossed my mind, but only for fleeting seconds. After the shock, my mind was set on keeping you. I told myself, "Children are a blessing from God. This is my baby. I'm going to keep it." Then came one of the most glorious and precious times in my life. (However, it was nowhere near the easiest.)

One day, a few months into my pregnancy, I heard God speak to me in my heart. He reminded me that you were not my baby, but His. He gave you life, not me. That was the changing point. That was the time I began to consider adoption.

Your adoption was carefully orchestrated by God. Through a miraculous series of events that your parents have told you about, God showed me that your parents were handpicked by Him. By God's graciousness I was allowed to be a part of that decision. To meet your parents, to talk to them and to tell them that in just six weeks they were to be parents was one of the most precious times in my life.

1

The decision wasn't always easy. People don't understand adoption, let alone open adoption. In the mid-eighties abortion was high, and open adoptions were new and frightening. Most people were supportive, but very few understood. In fact, a friend said to me once, "If you didn't want this baby, why didn't you abort it? You can be the woman of the nineties. You can have a baby and a career."

How do I make people understand? I wanted you very much. Numerous nights I cried over you, over the loss I would feel when we said good-bye. But I loved you too much to keep you. You see, I couldn't be both a mother and a father to you. In trying to do so I felt I would only be half the mother you deserved. You see, I loved you so much I wanted the very best for you. Your parents are it. You are the answer to their prayers, and they are the answer to mine.

Your parents have allowed me to have contact with you over the years — to watch you grow, to get letters and pictures, and to even meet you. Because of the parents God chose for you and His incredible mercy, we can have a relationship today.

Love,
Your birth mother

Teresa Eklund is a fashion designer. After finishing design school and working for other companies for a few years, she opened her own studio and dress shop specializing in formal wear. She lives in her home state of Ohio with her husband of two years. They are enthusiasts of a variety of music and also enjoy playing with their cat, Leo.

Her Choice, Our Blessing

by Carole Nordstrom

Good Morning, God!

Thank You for giving me another day of life. Help me to accomplish what You want of me today. Help me to be the kind of parent You want me to be. After all, we have dedicated our children to You!

You continue to amaze me with Your love for my family. Your hand in my life is so evident. Every good thing I have is because of You. Thank You.

Thanks for listening to my plea for a child! That was the longest prayer I've ever prayed. Eight years is a long time to wait for a child. At times I thought You were cruel, making me wait—suffering the pain of empty arms. Oh, God, it hurt so much! Nothing in my life has ever been as painful as those empty arms.

But Your timing is impeccable! Just when I couldn't stand it any longer, we met Terry. Not only are we blessed with her child, Angela; we are blessed by her example of unconditional and selfless love. Please, God, give her peace about her decision to place her daughter with us. Give her security in knowing that she did the best thing for her child.

It still makes me smile every time I think of how You got us together. To put total strangers together in such a perfect and glorious way is nothing short of a miracle! Terry is so special to us. I'm so grateful to You for our friendship and love for each other.

Thank You for Terry. Thanks for giving her the grace she needs to be the birth mom in her daughter's life. Thank You for filling her with love—for You, for Angela, for us. Give her joy as she continues to have a special relationship with Angela.

Angela is proud of the fact that she has two mommies. Thank You for her acceptance and adaptability. The concept

3

of adoption is tough for a young, immature mind to grasp. But again, Your love broke through. Thank You for giving her understanding of a tough fact of her life. Angela is well adjusted and loved by her adopted family, as well as her birth family. Please help her to grow up loving You. Help her to have peace in knowing that Terry loves her dearly.

And just when I thought it didn't get any better than this, You blessed us again, with Taylor! Another adoption was something I didn't think was in our future, but we applied at the agency anyway. I'm so glad we did. Oh, God, You do beautiful work! Taylor is just as pretty and sweet as Angela. They are so different, yet so alike. Taylor is such a joy! Thank You for touching her little four-pound body when she was lying in intensive care. I'm so grateful for how her tiny life is touching my life.

Thank You for Teresa, Taylor's birth mother. It's so evident that You are in her life. She's so young, yet so responsible. Her family plays such a big part in her life. Thank You for giving that family wisdom and peace to make this tough decision. Again, I stand in awe of Your power as You found the perfect match. Teresa is an extraordinary teenager. Her love for Taylor is evident. I'm thrilled that we have the opportunity to again build a relationship with Teresa as we did with Terry.

Please bless Teresa with joy and excitement for life. Give her an increased awareness of her youth. Walk closely with her through the rough days when she cries. Comfort her and give her peace in knowing that we love her daughter more than she can imagine. Keep her close to You.

As Taylor grows, give us wisdom to guide her as she learns to deal with her differences. From the outside looking in, people may think she has a lot to overcome because she's adopted and of mixed race. But from where I stand, she has already accomplished more than most adults. She's a strong little girl. Thank You for her health and sweet disposition. Thank You for her beauty. Please give her wisdom to understand what You have for her as she deals with the harsh, sometimes cruel world. And give her peace knowing that her birth mother loves her an immeasurable amount.

Two young lives are dependent on my care, love and nurturing. Two little pairs of eyes watch me, learning about life from my actions. Two youthful sets of ears hear me saying so much. Please, God, give me wisdom to speak truth and love. Let my actions be pure and my example what You want it to be.

Two tender lives were placed in our care for a special reason. Your ways are perfect. Please continue to shower our little family with wisdom and love, provision and confidence.

Father, You adopted us into Your royal family. It's awesome to realize that Terry and Teresa are our sisters in Your family. Thank You for cradling us in Your arms, holding us close when we have heartaches. I am most appreciative of the fact that You take the time to be involved in our lives so personally. May we all bring glory to You in all we do and say.

I love You, dear Father! ❧

> *Carole Nordstrom directs a teen mothers program for Youth for Christ International. Her husband, Dave, also is a staff member. The Nordstroms have two children and live in Michigan. Mrs. Nordstrom enjoys writing and taking quiet walks around the lake near their home.*

Somebody Loves You

by Stephanie O'Dell

Classic movies and classic books.

They filled my spare time, as a dreaming, love-seeking adolescent. And after thousands of hours of stories, I set out on my own, determined to find romance—the wonderful acceptance and love so many of my fictional characters had discovered.

All I found was classic guilt.

I raced through several heartbreaking relationships. I reluctantly agreed with a guitar-playing boyfriend to abort my only child. And I married a man twelve years my senior, expecting him to be "my everything."

Needless to say, as the men in my life rejected me, I rejected myself. Dreams of finding true love faded fast. I could not forgive myself for idolizing men and being promiscuous, and certainly I could not forgive myself for ending my baby's life. Soon my dreams and I fell, shattered.

Finally, I cried to God.

"Please show me that somebody loves me and will never leave me! I'm tired of hurting and want someone to love me for a lifetime—to know me and accept me."

God answered my cry for love and healing by giving me peace and forgiveness. He seared two short Scriptures into my mind and heart to confirm that He would never leave me or reject me, no matter what it was I had done!

Jesus said, "The one who comes to Me I will by no means cast out" (John 6:37). And God also said, "I will dwell in them [us] and walk among them [us]. I will be their God, and they shall be My people" (2 Corinthians 6:16).

Unlike anything else I had read, God's words spoke life and hope and possibility for true love in my life. Unbelievably, the One who created the universe wanted to be connected to me! Without hesitation, He accepted me just as I was, without my having to be thin or pretty—without my having to be anything. The only condition to my receiving God's love and forgiveness was accepting His Son Jesus as my Lord and Savior.

Freedom and joy came into my life when I handed over to Jesus the guilt of putting men first in my life instead of putting God first. Jesus took all that sin and gave me a new beginning.

"As far as the east is from the west, so far has He [God] removed our transgressions from us" (Psalm 103:12).

At first I had a hard time believing that God forgave me for the abortion. But God's consistent and powerful love said, *"You are forgiven."* With my past sins wiped away, God was able to fill the empty places created by the old dreams.

Today, I no longer refer to fictional characters when considering a future mate. I have no desire to fantasize about meeting "Mr. Perfect" either. Jesus is perfect, and God's love is more important to me now. I trust Him with my life, and I know He will never leave me.

God is simply amazing, and one of the most amazing things I've learned about my God is that He truly and faithfully loves me, as He loves every human He's created.

He authored love and He authored life.

His Book is nonfiction. His Son is prehistory. His love endures forever. ‏❧

Stephanie O'Dell has served as a counselor at two pregnancy care centers and now works on a CPC Board where she lives in Northern Illinois.
She received her bachelor of arts from the State University of New York and her master of arts in nineteenth-century American Literature from Miami University in Oxford, Ohio. Ms. O'Dell studied English at the University of London in England. One of her favorite memories is driving from New York to California in a pickup truck with her dog, Cimmeron, in 1983.

Margaret's Story

by Margaret Young

It was September 1975, my first year in high school. My mind was filled with dreams and high expectations.

I had long anticipated this time and really considered myself very close to being grown up. It was all so exciting! I was allowed new privileges—staying out later, going out with friends who could drive, and most importantly, boyfriends! Like most fifteen-year-old girls, I had a strong desire to feel special and important to someone. Yes, I knew my mother and my family loved me very much, but I was looking for a different kind of love.

A guy two years older than me named Perry was in two of my classes. He seemed to make the room come alive when he entered. He was funny, extremely cute, a talented artist and a member of the football team. I really liked him a lot, but I was not sure if I wanted to take a chance and let him know. What if the feelings were not mutual? I would be so embarrassed. It turned out that I did not have to make that decision. I was having difficulty with an art project, and he offered to help. Soon he began walking me to my classes and finally asked if he could come to my house to see me.

I was excited and nervous at the same time. What in the world would we talk about, what would I wear, and what would I do with my hair? It was not as bad as I thought it would be. It was amazing to me that our conversation flowed so easily. We shared a lot of the same interests—music, movies and a desire to go to college. I liked him more now than before. What surprised me most was his genuine interest in *me!*

We began to talk on the phone and spend lots of time together. I knew nothing about football, but I attended all the games to watch him play. I enjoyed his attention, and it felt nice that others viewed us as a couple.

I had not given much thought to what I would do if the subject of "sex" came up. Other boys I had liked expected sex to be a part of the relationship. I resented that kind of pressure but thought that perhaps it would be different with Perry—at least I hoped so, but deep inside I did not think it would be.

When the subject did come up, part of me was disappointed and part of me felt that maybe I was being unrealistic. I thought that if I really wanted a relationship, I needed to accept that sex would go with it.

Sex became a regular part of my relationship with Perry. I did not consider using birth control because I never made a conscious decision to continue having sex. After a few months things started to change. I did not feel as excited as I felt earlier in the relationship. We began to have heated arguments and to break up often. By this time, I was sixteen and he was eighteen. Although we still had fun times, the relationship had become very stressful and draining for both of us. And then to make matters worse, I was pregnant.

I was devastated! What was I going to do? How could I possibly tell my mother? More than anything I did not want to disappoint her. And what about my plans for college? I could not even begin to imagine how Perry and I could care for a child. This was not supposed to happen! With things the way they were between us, how long could I count on him being there for me and this baby?

Perry was scared but seemed almost happy about it. I felt anger toward him. This was all his fault. If only he had not asked me to have sex with him. But I knew in my heart that I was also responsible. I could have said "no." I guess at the time I felt I did not have a choice. But I did have a choice, and I chose to say "yes."

I mustered up the courage to tell an adult cousin, who told my mother. To my amazement, my mother was very supportive, encouraging and calm. I began to feel that the only way to make things right again was to have an abortion. I went to a clinic and scheduled an appointment for the following week. The morning I was going to have the abortion, I realized I could not go through with it. I told my mother I had decided to have the baby. Perry made a commitment to her and to me that he would do all that he could to support me and the baby.

I was about to embark on one of the most challenging and difficult events of my life, and I was terrified. Although I knew some of my friends were having sex, I felt a sense of guilt because *I* had become pregnant. Everyone would be able to see in me what they could only suspect in others. It was difficult to go to school when I first started showing and people would stare at me and whisper. But I was determined to finish school.

My relationship with Perry was pretty much the same—on again, off again. But at least he was still around. I was seventeen years old and seven months pregnant when I finished my junior year of high school in June of 1977. The baby was due on August 12. I was getting really excited. The due date came and went, and I was beginning to think this baby would never arrive.

I was in the hospital being treated for a urinary tract infection when I went into labor. The birth of my child was imminent.

My mother was at the hospital with me, but nurses would not permit her to be present at the birth because she had not taken childbirth classes. Although Perry and I continued to communicate for the baby's sake, our relationship was all but dissolved. I felt very alone and afraid. After all, I was only seventeen years old and never remembered even being in the hospital before.

After seventeen hours of labor, on August 27, 1977, I gave birth to the most beautiful girl I had ever laid eyes on. The minute I saw her I knew I made the right decision.

The responsibility I felt for caring for such a precious little life was awesome. But with my mother's guidance I learned how to be a loving, responsible mother. I returned to school a month after the baby was born and graduated in June 1978. At this time, Perry was no longer involved in our lives.

I found a job as a clerk in a publishing company. I also attended a business school at night. I was determined to provide a good life for my child and myself.

Although things were basically going well for me, a void existed in my life. I believed life consisted of something more than what I was experiencing. My sister had recently become a Christian and shared her experience with me. I realized this was what I had been looking for. I asked Jesus Christ to come into my heart, and my life has never been the same.

One of my prayers was that my daughter would have the benefit of a father's love. I realized how important it was for a child to have a father because I did not grow up with my father involved in my life. God answered my prayer beyond my wildest dreams. When my daughter was two years old, I met, fell in love with and married the most wonderful man. Not only did he fall in love with me; he fell in love with my daughter and has reared her as his own child.

I had no idea sixteen years ago that things would work out for my daughter and me the way they did. Perhaps right now you do not know how things will work out for you in the next few months. Like I was many years ago, you may be feeling anxious and afraid. But I pray that my story will give you hope and courage to choose the gift of life for the child growing inside of you. I also trust that the same God who made a way for me will make a way for you. ॐ

Margaret Young is office manager of Capitol Hill Crisis Pregnancy Center. She and her husband, William, a pastor, have four daughters and live in the Washington, D.C., metropolitan area. Mrs. Young is active in women's ministry as a Bible study teacher and seminar speaker. She also enjoys cooking and writing poetry.

Unconditional Love

by Melinda Delahoyde

*W*hat was it like when our son, Will, was born?

Although I have answered that question many times in the last ten years, it always catches me off guard and sends me back to the days when we were brand new parents of a baby boy with Down's syndrome.

There were so many conflicting feelings during those months: anger, pain, hope, sadness, love. We felt them all—like every parent—and I had so many questions. Will he walk? Can we have other children? How will our families react? What will his future be like? What will I say when the other children call him "retarded"? So many feelings and questions, but so few answers. Our life was in chaos.

Still, throughout those days, two thoughts were engraved in my heart: God loves me and I love my baby. To us, Will was the most adorable child in the world. Through all the doctors visits, genetic tests and therapy sessions, I loved this baby. Being his mother was a joy which nothing could diminish.

But I wish that during Will's first few months I could have read an article like the one I recently wrote about him and a trip to a store. I would have seen that God loved this child, too, and could use his life in a unique way. I would have realized that life would go on after the pain and grief.

Most of all, however, I would have understood more clearly what I found to be true during those early days: no matter what the challenges or the hurts—some problems just cannot be fixed—our love for Will and his love for us will always be greater. It is never just the cold, hard facts of living with a handicapped child that stare me in the face. I face those facts with God's love and an overwhelming love for our son, and that will always be enough. It's a good life for our family—real happiness for all of us.

A reminder from God about the value of life prompted the article I mentioned.

Saturday morning at the grocery store—the prospect couldn't be more unpleasant for me to contemplate. The grocery store is never my first choice of places to spend time, and it is hardly the place I would expect God to illustrate one of His deep truths. But this is exactly what He did one day for me and my son.

We badly needed help that morning. The schedules of four small children and a busy husband had left me no time for shopping and no food in the house. At least there was one bright spot on the horizon—I could spend a few hours with Will. Like most nine-year-olds, he is energetic, independent and full of new ideas.

So off we went to the store. I was looking grim and determined to face the crowds, and Will was looking forward to all the forbidden foods he would finagle from me. What a contrast we were that morning. I carried the burdens of the world on my shoulders, while Will was off to a great adventure. I could not realize then that I would be the one to enjoy the adventure.

Will is usually enthusiastic about everything he does. For him there are always people to meet and friends to make. He simply loves life and people. As we walked the aisles of the store, though, it was obvious that not everyone shared his excitement. Women, with toddlers in tow, and men, mostly looking lost, were rustling to accomplish their missions. Nobody wanted to be there, and there was not a smile to be found—except Will's.

As my son passed by each of those people, a transformation took place. Shoppers who had barely noticed me would stop their carts and chat with Will, usually about ten steps behind me and looking for his favorite cookies. It is difficult to ignore Will's entreaties. Not only does he stop to say hello, but he also introduces himself and shakes hands.

Even so, the contrast was amazing. I would pass people in the aisle and the response was usually the same: no smile and maybe a nod. Then Will would come along and their faces would light up. Men and women who would not even say hello to me stopped to tell Will their life stories.

I decided I would put Will's social skills to the test. I purposely maneuvered my cart so that we would come face to face with the worst of this bunch of shoppers. I looked for the sourest face and the gloomiest disposition. The results were always the same: a blank stare for me and avid enthusiasm for Will.

I set my sight on one particular woman. She was one tough character, and I was sure no one could make her crack. As she headed for the check-out counter, I grabbed Will so we could be in line behind her. Not even Will, I was sure, could bring a smile to her face.

I was wrong. As Will began to help her unload her groceries onto the conveyer belt, that gruff exterior melted away. In the course of several minutes in line, we learned how many children this woman had, why she needed particular grocery items, and what kind of weather we could expect that day.

I left the store feeling very differently than when I entered. I was astonished at the impact one nine-year-old boy had made upon the lives of those people. For just a few moments, Will, just by being himself, had brought gladness and affection to the lives of some very gloomy grocery shoppers. I had not been able to do it, and neither had anyone else in that store. Will had done it just by being himself.

Often we look upon those who have special needs in our society as people to whom we can give our money, time and pity. I learned that morning that we are not the ones who make the greatest contributions. It is not just a matter of "us" giving to "them." My son, and so many others like him, make the very highest quality contribution to the lives of all of us. They give us the gift of love. 🙠

A resident of North Carolina, Melinda Delahoyde is an author whose care for handicapped children is recognized nationwide. She serves Special Olympics as a volunteer and vocal fan. Mrs. Delahoyde received her bachelor of arts degree in philosophy from the University of California in 1976 and was graduated cum laude in 1979 from Trinity Divinity School with a master of arts in philosophy of religion. She and her husband, Bill, have four children.

Fatherhood

by Richard Renzi

It has been said that "man is the saddest of creatures, torn between having his feet bound to the earth and his heart drawn to the heavens." How many times have you asked yourself, *Why did this happen to me? Why did God let this happen?*

It's strange how God works. He allows us to make our own mistakes. He does this so that we may pull together and help each other. Along the way we can develop ourselves.

As a man, it's okay to feel strongly about what is going to happen to your baby. It's okay to become involved. Go with your heart. Commit yourself, all that you are, no matter how undeveloped or uneducated you may feel about yourself, to protecting your baby. You are born with these qualities. It is within you.

As much as we may all think this world has changed and as much as the roles of women and men have become similar, our basic roles and desires remain unchanged. Women still naturally nurture and care greater than any force on earth. A man's natural inclination is to protect and provide.

God created you as a man with a natural chemistry and desire to protect your baby, and He has also given you something else to help you provide for your baby: determination, a potentially powerful force.

So often today, however, a father will hold back his natural protection and stifle determination. What is left is a mother, struggling her very best to raise, teach and provide for her little one. It is hard for all of us to make it on our own, but it is especially hard for a mother to make it while caring for a baby.

Many women are strong and find the courage to have their babies, but many cannot face this challenge. They become consumed with despair over tough times that may lay ahead and the thought of their male companion's empty promises. They envision a future without support or compassion. It is at this point that a baby's life is vulnerable to abortion.

Before going along with a doctor or nurse, many women will look to their male companion to see whether he is willing to protect and to provide for his child. All that is really required is a little courage, a little compassion. Fathers who run or hold back their support contribute more than their share to abortion.

Often a doctor will eagerly replace an uncommitted father. For a fee, a few doctors and nurses show false compassion, justify their task and make easy work of a defenseless baby. Refusing defense and support, the father allows his child to be taken.

If your baby could talk, he or she may beg you, "Father, please. I know we are in trouble, but please help me. Your shoulders are strong. I need to learn the lessons that only a father can instinctively teach. I want to learn the lessons of your youth. I need to know how when you were young you may have been scared or hurt. I want to know how you grew in strength and courage and were able to become a man. I need a father to help me with my school, my sports, with my music lessons. I'm willing to share my youth with you."

Remember, the determination of a new father is very powerful. Put it to good use. Be still and ponder your own situation. Put it upon yourself to solve the hows and whys. Put off sleep. Don't rest until you find a way to make it. When you do this, what you will find is your own spirit.

Take your spirit, your energy and your determination and concentrate it. Focus it on supporting your new baby. Work hard. You will earn enough to be a good provider. Force your mind and heart to draw upon your resources and your relationships. God will not allow you to go unaided.

God often works through people. He uses their talents and energies to solve problems and provide answers and solutions. He uses their eyes, ears, hands and feet to intercede and provide help. So don't be afraid to get proper counsel from others. Be sure they have the benefit of age, experience and character, but include the whole world as your audience. Share your story of courage with anyone who will listen.

Many of us share the same responsibilities of providing for our children. This common cause and purpose will help you to meet people and develop more working relationships. Since God works through people, the more people who understand your purpose and objective, the more probability God has of helping you.

Also know that as you learn and grow in parenthood, your child will benefit from your teachings. A child listens to a father differently. A father's influences and his teachings are very important to the development of a child. Choose to be there for your little one.

Be there to see your baby's first tears, perhaps a gift of thanks from your child for making the tough decision to help him or her be born and for having the courage to just say you're going to try. Accept your baby's tears of thanks for standing strong and for not running. Take hold of your baby and whisper, "As long as you breathe, as long as you need me, I will be here for you."

You can draw upon this new life for the strength you need to pull you through. If a day's frustration causes you to want to quit, recall the eyes of your little one. Then gather yourself, and face your daily challenges.

Help bring your children into this world and raise them. Let them be your joy—your rock, your foundation—not your burden. They will give you back your youth, your innocence. Welcome your children into the world and strive to be a good father. For now, plan to comfort them and keep them safe.

Above all, know that where there is desire and determination, especially for the life of a child, friends, family and even acquaintances will flock to your aid. When you have tried as hard as you can to be a good father, and you have done all you can to protect and provide, rest yourself and ask for help. ❧

Richard Renzi and his wife have eight children and live in the Washington, D.C., area. He is president of his own group of insurance companies and works with three youth sports associations. He was an outstanding high school athlete and went on to become captain of his university's football team. Mr. Renzi now keeps in shape by running daily and by playing raquetball.

Birth and Rebirth —
A Time to Rejoice

by Pam Harmon, ICCE

A miracle. From the first kick inside your womb to the first cry to the first word, the child you are expecting is a miracle.

Few joys in life match the joy you will feel on the day your baby comes into the world. Everyone around you at that moment will be excited. And as you hold your little one during the first weeks and months, any childbirth pain you may have had will become a faint memory, lessened by God's most precious creation, a new life.

But babies aren't the only creatures who may receive life anew. God offers everyone a fresh start. When we turn our lives over to God and are forgiven through Jesus for everything we've ever done wrong, we get to begin a new life. And God's angels rejoice. "I say to you, there is joy in the presence of the angels of God over one sinner who repents," Jesus said in Luke 15:10.

Difficult choices will develop as we try to live the way that God tells us in the Bible. One of Jesus' early followers, Paul, wrote, "I consider that the sufferings of this present time are not worthy to be compared with the glory which shall be revealed in us" (Romans 8:18). The same can be said for us today. The problems we have on earth are nothing in light of the joy we can experience by being one of God's children.

A certified childbirth educator, Pam Harmon is director of the Teen Parent Program at a pregnancy care center in Washington, D.C. She and her husband, Mark, have two children, Andrew, 10, and Lindsay, 7. Mrs. Harmon is a graduate of Westmount College in Santa Barbara, California. Active in urban minis-

*tries with her husband, she says that a highlight of
her life is participating in a baby's birth. She also
enjoys the outdoors.*

*   *   *   *   *   *   *   *   *   *   *   *   *   *   *   *   *   *

If you are not God's child, not saved, you can be at this
moment. *But what must I do to be saved?* you may be asking.

The Bible records this question as falling from the lips of a
Philippian jailer. It was his responsibility to guard the imprisoned Silas and Paul, two early Christian missionaries. While
these men were praying, worshiping and praising God in the
presence of their fellow prisoners, an earthquake opened their
cells and loosed their chains. The frightened jailer, believing the
men had escaped and he had failed to carry out his duties, was
ready to kill himself. The men, however, stopped him, saying
that no one had left.

That must have been amazing to the jailer. Why would anyone imprisoned not leap at the chance to escape? Either these
men were crazy, or they had something he was lacking—
something he wanted in his own life. When he asked, "What
must I do to be saved?" he might have been asking, "What must
I do to be set free?" Perhaps he recognized a bondage in his life
that was a more sure captor than cell bars—the bondage called
sin.

Sin is anything in our lives that shuts us away from a full
and satisfying relationship with God. It hinders our potential to
be all He wants us to be and to do all He wants us to do. Romans 3:23 says, "All have sinned and fall short of the glory of
God." Therefore, each of us has to face this choice at some time
in our lives: the choice to serve God or to serve sin.

By choosing to be lost to sin, we gain death. By becoming
a child of God, we gain life. Paul's answer to the wondering
jailer was, "Believe on the Lord Jesus Christ, and you will be
saved, you and your household" (Acts 16:31).

Who Is the Lord Jesus Christ?

In today's age of enlightenment, new physics, and spiritual-
ism, Jesus is often taken to be no more than one of the world's
great teachers. He is simply one of the "Christs," another

Buddha or Confucius, . . . *A* way to God-consciousness. Jesus, however, did not proclaim Himself as *A* way to God-consciousness. Rather, He said He was *The* way to God. "I am the way, the truth, and the life. No one comes to the Father except through Me" (John 14:6).

The hardest thing for any of us to do is to let go of our own wills and let God act in and through us. We tend to think we can figure things out, that we can do for ourselves. It goes against our grain to accept another individual's sacrifice for us. We don't want to be in anyone's debt—let alone when that One is God. And yet, God came to earth in the Person of His Son to bleed for a world that rejected Him in favor of serving sin and death. Why? "For God so loved the world that He gave His only begotten Son, that whoever believes in Him should not perish but have everlasting life" (John 3:16).

God didn't call back the death sentence He had pronounced in the Garden of Eden. Rather, He suffered it for us. And He said that if we would accept His sacrifice, as surely as Jesus had been raised from death, He would give us new life too. And you can have this new life, this new freedom, right now.

What Must *You* Do to Be Saved?

Recognize that you are a sinner. Without Christ, we are all slaves to sin. None of us, no matter how good or moral we are, is worthy of what God in Christ has done for us. "For the wages of sin is death, but the gift of God is eternal life in Christ Jesus our Lord" (Romans 6:23).

Believe on the Lord Jesus Christ. Believe that He is who He said He is—God in the flesh, who chose to die to take away your sin so that you can live forever. "But as many as received Him, to them He gave the right to become children of God, to those who believe in His name: who were born, not of blood, nor of the will of the flesh, nor of the will of man, but of God" (John 1:12-13).

Repent of your sins. Choose to turn away from sin and toward God. "If we confess our sins, He is faithful and just to forgive us our sins and to cleanse us from all unrighteousness" (1 John 1:9).

Open your heart to Jesus Christ as your Lord and Savior. Jesus has said, "Behold, I stand at the door and knock. If anyone hears My voice and opens the door, I will come in to him and dine with him, and he with Me" (Revelation 3:20). Accept Jesus' great sacrifice for you, realizing that He is the only One who can save you. In Him alone is the strength we need to turn from our sins and let God live through our lives.

You might pray a prayer like this:

Father, thank You for caring so much about me that You sent Your Son Jesus to die for me. I know that I am a sinner and that I don't deserve what You have done for me. But I accept that You have done it because You love me and because You want a relationship with me. I welcome You into my heart and into my life, and I pray that You will work in me from this minute on. In Jesus' name, Amen.

How Can You Grow in the Faith You Have Just Professed?

1. Read the Bible. It is the Word of God, which will tell you more about Him and about His plan for your life.

2. Spend time in prayer—*worshiping* God, *confessing* wrongs in your life, *asking* for help and guidance, *listening* for His answers.

3. Join a strong, Bible-believing church. Encouragement from other Christians is important. "But, speaking the truth in love, we may grow up in all things into Him who is the head— Christ—from whom the whole body, joined and knit together by what every joint supplies, according to the effective working by which every part does its share, causes growth of the body for the edifying of itself in love" (Ephesians 4:15-16).

4. Tell other people about the new life you have found in Christ, and invite them to become part of God's family too. ❧

Selected Scriptures and Daily Devotions

An Invitation for You

I remember a dense fog I had to drive through on my way to teach years ago when my husband was seriously ill. When I left for my classroom that late-autumn morning, it was so murky I had to drive by instinct on the back road. After several moments of the car's crawling pace, I knew a stop sign should be just ahead. Ah, there it was.

As I edged the car forward, I decided the fog wouldn't be as dense on top of the overpass. At least I'd be able to see from there. I inched to the top, expecting only greater visibility. Instead I was treated to an incredible sight. The little valleys surrounding the expressway were filled with pink mist rather than depressing fog. And above the mysterious pink haze were the sun's rays, showing through purple and orange clouds.

The cars on the road below crept through the murk I had escaped. If only they could have this view!

When I had to leave the overpass and descend into the fog again, the memory of the beautiful scene went with me. I continued to school, strangely refreshed as I realized beauty would come after my personal fog too. I just hadn't made it to a place where I could see above the bewilderment.

You may be in a fog of your own, traveling an unfamiliar road, considering choices never faced before and unable to "drive by instinct." Perhaps you decided to give your baby life and saw the incredible view from the overpass, but the fog has returned with thoughts of whether to keep your child or entrust him or her to another family.

Trust me. Beauty will come after the fog. You just haven't made it to a place where you can see above it.

While I share thoughts about pregnancy and birth in the following pages, you'll read about my Kentucky background and family. The devotions are accompanied by Bible passages.

I hope you'll write your own notes and prayers in the margin. Later you'll be amazed at your feelings and emotional progress. If you're sending your baby into another family, you might even send this book along for that time when he or she may ask about you. If you're rearing the child, tuck this away to share together later.

If you haven't used a devotional book before, you may be a little unsure how to begin. Here are five steps that have helped me get more out of the readings.

1. Read it through. I hope you'll enjoy the stories that I tell. One of the joys of having lived this long is that I have lots of experiences.

2. Think about what I've said. Do you agree? Disagree? What do you wish I'd written about?

3. Read the Scriptures highlighted and several more before and after. That way you'll have a clearer picture of what was happening.

4. Make a connection between what I've written and what is going on in your own life.

5. Pick one aspect to think about throughout the day. Don't try to chew on everything. Think about just one point in my story or in the Scriptures that hits your particular need.

So let's get started on this new adventure. If you like, imagine that we're sitting together on the sofa as I tell you some of my experiences.

God bless you in the days ahead. &

> Sandra Picklesimer Aldrich
> Colorado Springs, 1993

Daily Devotions

$\mathcal{T}$hen the word of the LORD
came to me, saying:

"Before I formed you in the
womb I knew you;
Before you were born I
sanctified you;
I ordained you a prophet to the
nations."

Jeremiah 1:4-5

Before Our Time

Jeremiah 1:4-5

Before my husband, Don, and I were married, he often substitute taught in his hometown eighty miles away. One lunch period he wrote to me: "I look at these seventh-grade girls and wonder what our own little Holly will be like." Then he described how he hoped her personality would develop.

It would be nine more years before we could use the name for our daughter. During that time of waiting, we had only dreams to attach to a yet-unseen person.

But in the first chapter of Jeremiah God declares that not only had He known the prophet before he was born, but He had, in fact, been the One who formed him. This was no accident of nature. And to make it even better, Jeremiah, even as an unborn child, was sanctified—or set apart—for God's righteous purpose.

Each person God creates can claim these verses. As individuals, we are an important part of His master plan before our birth. And although we may not grow up to be a prophet or leader, God values us. Even with our faults, He has something wonderful in mind for each of us.🐦

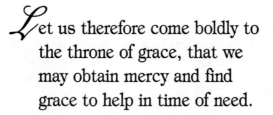

*L*et us therefore come boldly to
the throne of grace, that we
may obtain mercy and find
grace to help in time of need.

Hebrews 4:16

Bold Forgiveness
Hebrews 4:16

The woman waited until everyone had left before she approached me after the Bible study. Quiet and apologetic, she tugged at her sleeves as she told of her long-ago decision to abort her fourth child.

"I can't ask for forgiveness," she whispered. "I knew what I was doing, but I thought it would be better for the family. I planned to have the 'procedure,' as the doctor called it, and get on with life. I hadn't planned to feel so empty. . . ."

The woman didn't look as though she had ever approached anything boldly, but I opened the Scriptures to Hebrews 4.

"This means we can confidently approach a throne of *grace*, not judgment," I said. "Because of what Jesus did for us when He took our place on the Cross, we may boldly ask for mercy, especially when we are in distress. Mercy is what allows God to help the miserable. And we can expect to receive that mercy, along with a helping of God's loving-kindness, once we have asked for His forgiveness."

As I talked, the woman watched me carefully, wanting very much to believe my words. When I hugged her and started to pray, the grieving mother poured out years of pain onto my shoulder. Asking for and accepting God's forgiveness finally gave her the peace she needed. ❧

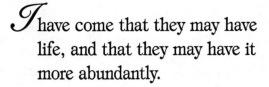

$\mathcal{I}$have come that they may have
life, and that they may have it
more abundantly.

Jesus
John 10:10b

Accepting Abundant Life
John 10:10b

The young expectant mother asked to talk with me after church. I quietly waited as she twisted her wedding rings. Finally, she stammered, "I'm afraid God's going to kill my baby because I had an abortion when I was sixteen."

I grabbed her in one of my Kentucky hugs and just let her cry. When she was quiet, I talked about God's forgiveness and the abundant life He wants to give us.

Satan loves situations like this where the person remains trapped by past sin. As long as he can strangle us with our guilt, we can't accept the joy and freedom the Lord wants to give. The Enemy is very much like a thief who comes into a pen to steal sheep. The thief steals, kills and destroys. He comes for purely selfish motives.

But Jesus came to not only protect His sheep—us—but to give us an abundant life, full of His joy and His power. With the Good Shepherd, the sheep have peace because Jesus does not come to our hearts for selfish reasons. He comes to give, not to get.

Christ came to Earth to offer us eternal life and to make our earthly one better. By His words and actions He opposed anything that might diminish it. He can help us break free of Satan's hold on our minds.

*F*or You formed my inward
parts;
You covered me in my mother's
womb.
I will praise You, for I am
fearfully and wonderfully
made,
Marvelous are Your works,
And that my soul knows very
well.
My frame was not hidden from
You,
When I was made in secret,
And skillfully wrought in the
lowest parts of the earth.

David
Psalm 139:13-15

Wonderfully Made
Psalm 139:13-15

When I taught high schoolers about ancient cultures, we often talked about the Roman custom of abandoning unwanted newborns on a hillside. The students would demand to know how a culture could do such a heartless thing. I'd shrug and say, "We do the same thing here. They killed their babies *after* birth; we kill ours *before* birth." Suddenly I had their full attention.

In Psalm 139, it's clear that God made each of us as an individual physical being. The word "covered" actually means "interwoven." That is, the cells, bones, veins and arteries are all woven together. The thought is repeated in verse 15 where "wrought" presents the idea of being embroidered with various colors within the darkness of the womb.

Here we see that life begins at conception. God fashioned us while we were in our mother's womb and prescribed the custom design for each of us according to His purpose. God does not analyze personal worth as man does, for He looks beyond our feeble frames to the picture within. Even the most tragic circumstances can be overruled or redirected to good by the providence of God—if we will look through His eyes. 🙢

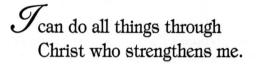

$\mathcal{I}$ can do all things through
Christ who strengthens me.

Apostle Paul
Philippians 4:13

Strength, Not Fear

Philippians 4:13

Our Tuesday night Lamaze classes were coming to an end. Within a few more weeks, eight little human beings would be kicking the air instead of our rib cages. As final preparation, the instructor showed the film of an actual birth.

Watching the on-screen mother panting at the right moments, we thought of our own soon-arriving deliveries. As the film ended and the instructor turned on the lights, a first-time mother gasped, "I can't do that!" She started to sob.

The tension was contagious; suddenly the rest of us had tears in our eyes too. Then the group's lone teenager, the one who had her sister as her birth coach, spoke. "I get real scared sometimes," she said. "But then I just remember that God's gonna help me. . . . Besides, it's a little late for us to back out of giving birth now."

We smiled a bit then. We knew she had chosen to give her baby up for adoption rather than accept the abortion her boyfriend demanded.

Within the next month, all eight babies arrived safely.

The teenager's no-nonsense humor comes to mind as I read Philippians 4:13. Paul declared the source of his strength just after saying he had learned to be content whether he possessed much or little. He also had learned he could do those things God asked because He would give him the necessary power.

"God's gonna help me" is a nice reminder for us all.

$\mathcal{A}$nd I will pray the Father,
and He will give you another
Helper, that He may abide
with you forever.

Jesus
John 14:16

Help from the Holy Spirit
John 14:16

My errands had gone fairly well, even with three-month-old Holly in my left arm, my purse slung over my shoulder, and purchases in my left hand while I clutched twenty-month-old Jay with my right.

As we approached an escalator, I let go of my toddler for a second to steady myself. Quickly I reached for Jay, but he stepped backward, unsure of getting on anything that moved. The escalator was taking me away as he stood watching. Before I had a chance to panic, an older couple walked up behind Jay. "Please grab his hand," I said. The couple nodded and brought my smiling little boy with them.

I think of that experience each time I read the words in John 14 spoken by Jesus to His disciples. After all, that's what the Holy Spirit does for us: He grabs our hand and helps us through scary times. The word translated "Helper" actually means "one called to the side of another to help." So as we ask for His help, He will comfort, strengthen and assist us. Jesus knew that soon He would be returning to heaven, having completed His work of dying on the Cross as a sacrifice for our sins. But before He left, He asked His Father to send a Helper who would remain with believers forever. In the Old Testament, the Holy Spirit visited people at various times, but often left them. Now at Jesus' request, He will never leave—and He will grab our hands along the way.

$\mathcal{A}$nd it happened, when Elizabeth heard the greeting of Mary, that the babe leaped in her womb; and Elizabeth was filled with the Holy Spirit.

Luke 1:41

Mysterious Fluttering

Luke 1:41

The mysterious moment when the elderly Elizabeth felt the movement of her unborn son, who would later be known as John the Baptist, is recorded only in the Gospel of Luke. Perhaps Luke, a doctor, was intrigued by the physical aspects of this phenomenon, but he reports that the child moved with such intensity that Elizabeth, under the guidance of the Holy Spirit, could offer the joyous encouragement her timid cousin needed. We don't know if this was the first time Elizabeth had felt the baby move, but we do know it was significant enough that it became a special moment.

Ask most mothers when they first felt their unborn baby's movements, and their countenance softens as they describe the experience. Even twenty years later, I remember I was sitting at my desk, greeting my students as they came into class. I was wearing a pale green dress and had a lacy white shawl over my shoulders. I held my breath as I felt the incredible tiny fluttering which seemed like butterfly wings beating deep within or the sensation when you gently touch your tongue to the inside of your cheek. That moment brought the most incredible knowledge: a real person was growing within the secret depths of my body. In that moment the same awe and joy which poured over Elizabeth—and surely every other mother throughout the ages—welled up in me. ❧

$\mathscr{T}$hen He said to His disciples,
"Therefore I say to you, do not
worry about your life, what
you will eat; nor about the
body, what you will put on.
Life is more than food, and the
body is more than clothing."

Jesus
Luke 12:22-23

The Most Important Possession

Luke 12:22-23

When Lisa was pregnant with her first child, she spent hours in a store's baby department, making a list of everything she wanted. She was especially determined to buy the best maple crib and matching dresser, noting that the accompanying youth bed was available. After all, she wanted her child to have the very best—not like her own childhood bed that had been a small mattress pushed into a corner of a tiled room.

Lisa had forgotten that her childhood was unhappy because of neglect and tension, not because she lacked nice things. Babies need love and security, not the biggest and the best in furniture and clothes.

In Luke, Jesus is saying we shouldn't concentrate on getting the unimportant things in life. Our time on earth is too precious to waste worrying about "things." The Bible tells us God has promised to provide everything we need. We need to put more confidence in our other blessings, like family.

Our little ones will be with us for only a short time. They will forget whether they had size one designer jeans or the most stylish crib. But they will remember, even subconsciously, whether they were loved and protected.

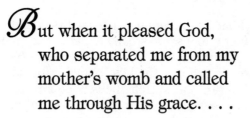

$\mathcal{B}$ut when it pleased God,
who separated me from my
mother's womb and called
me through His grace. . . .

Apostle Paul
Galatians 1:15

Set Apart by God
Galatians 1:15

Jay started running even before he was born. He kicked my ribs, punched my bladder and, as he braced his feet against my hip bones, stretched against my lungs until I thought I'd burst. Whenever we attended noisy family gatherings, he became even more active, as though he had a few things he wanted to say too.

Holly, on the other hand, liked finding a comfortable spot and settling in for several hours. I was always thumping my side to make her move so I could assure myself she was all right.

Those pre-birth personalities are still dominant. After college, Jay wants to travel the world, while Holly sets up a daycare center and plans her menus for the family get-togethers. I'm thankful both know that God can use each personality.

In Galatians, Paul realized that even before his birth, he had been set apart by God for a special work. He adds that God called him through His grace, referring to his conversion on the road to Damascus. Until that moment, he was actively persecuting Christians, convinced they were a fanatical group that was dangerous to Judaism. But Christ, in wonderful grace, saved him and sent him out to preach the faith he had tried to destroy.

Paul was changed from persecutor to preacher, but his personality and energy didn't change; they were just beautifully used for God's purposes. What a wonderful reminder: let's accept our children's personalities and teach them to use it for God's glory.

$\mathcal{T}$here is a lad here who has five barley loaves and two small fish, but what are they among so many?

Andrew
John 6:9

Unexpected Company

John 6:9

When Mindy was a child, unexpected company often arrived at dinnertime. As her mother greeted the guests, Mindy's job was to stir up another batch of cornbread to stretch the meal. At the table, Mindy's mother would give her a big wink which said, "Thanks!"

The disciples in John's story have a problem which can't be solved with extra cornbread: five thousand men and their families have shown up unexpectedly for dinner.

As Jesus watches the crowd approach, He asks Philip where they can buy bread since He wanted to see how His disciple would solve the problem. Philip doesn't have a solution; he just replies that even two-thirds of a man's yearly wages couldn't feed all the people.

In the middle of their discussion, another disciple, Andrew, steps forward with a little boy who has apparently offered his own food. But even as Andrew presents the gift, he belittles it, saying it isn't enough.

Jesus doesn't argue. He just gives Andrew instructions: "Make the people sit down." Then He takes the bread and fish, offers thanks and begins handing out the food.

Did the little boy's eyes grow wide as he watched his tiny lunch being multiplied? Did he wonder how Jesus did that? Was he surprised that the Lord used his gift to perform a miracle? Maybe he just stood there grinning. And maybe Jesus winked His thanks.

*W*hy are you cast down, O my
    soul?
And why are you disquieted
    within me?
Hope in God, for I shall yet
    praise Him
For the help of His
    countenance.

Psalm 42:5

Resting in the Lord

Psalm 42:5

Jill didn't understand why she was so depressed. She had a wonderful husband, a darling newborn son, terrific in-laws a loving and exciting church. So why these overwhelmingly sad feelings?

A visit to the doctor reminded her that her body was going through a time of adjustment after giving birth. Now she needed to be good to herself: eat nourishing foods, get as much rest as possible, stop worrying about the condition of the house and enjoy her husband and new son.

In Kentucky, we explain a person's temporary withdrawal from life with the non-judgmental expression that he "took to bed." Actually, I wish the rest of the culture would catch onto the concept that it's okay to rest and analyze our circumstances when we're discouraged. Often when we are "cast down," it takes time until we can lift our faces again. But an important part of our healing is knowing that we aren't alone. As we look to God, we see in Him encouragement to get us through any circumstance.

Even though Psalm 42 was written by King David and not by a woman who had just given birth, it still speaks to our hurts today. It is the prayer of a believer who struggled with doubt and depression but finally realized that everything he needed could be found in faith in God. ❧

*Y*et in all these things we are more than conquerors through Him who loved us. For I am persuaded that neither death nor life, nor angels nor principalities nor powers, nor things present nor things to come, nor height nor depth, nor any other created thing, shall be able to separate us from the love of God which is in Christ Jesus our Lord.

Apostle Paul
Romans 8:37-39

God's Invincible Power

The Sunday school teacher, wanting her class to understand God's protective power, asked, "What does 'principalities' mean?"

One eager little guy shot his hand into the air. "It's a whole bunch of school principals learning to be friends."

Well, not exactly. Principalities are the evil spirits that roam the earth, causing havoc. While we Christians often wrestle against them, we can be victorious because Christ has defeated them.

In his letter to the church at Rome, the Apostle Paul has named everything that has the potential to cause us trouble, but added that not even this list can separate us from the love of God. This is not presented in an attitude of conceit, but of confidence, as we are reminded of His ever-present love and strength.

Let's look at the list more closely. Death with all its terror can't separate us from God's love. Nor can life with all its temptations. Neither angels nor demons. No power, earthly or supernatural, will separate us. Nor will our present crises or the fears of the future. Neither height nor depth—those things, including occult forces, within space or the earth—can terrorize us.

Then to make sure that he is not missing anything, Paul adds "nor any other created thing." The outcome of Paul's search is that he can find *nothing* that can separate us from God's love, which is in Christ Jesus our Lord. And if Paul couldn't find anything, why should we make our own terror lists? Let's instead concentrate on God's love and power to help us be the men and women, and parents, He wants us to be.

51

$\mathcal{N}$ow may the God of hope fill
you with all joy and peace in
believing, that you may abound
in hope by the power of the
Holy Spirit.

Apostle Paul
Romans 15:13

Releasing the Past

Romans 15:13

Melinda and Paul were excited about becoming parents, but they were scared too. What if they made the same mistakes their folks had made? Melinda's mother had thought children needed only food, clothing and shelter. She hadn't understood the importance of encouragement and hugs. Paul's father had been an alcoholic. Even though he'd never physically abused his family, he was never available for them either. Paul had no idea how to be a father.

Wisely, the young couple presented their fears to their pastor. He first assured them their concerns weren't unusual. Then he directed them to Scripture passages showing that God parents us and will help us discover more about His loving role. Next, the pastor referred them to several books to help them sort through their childhood issues. Finally, he referred them to a church group led by couples who had successfully guided their own children into adulthood. The group helped others prepare for typical parenting situations and offered positive solutions.

Romans 15:13 is one verse the pastor suggested. Notice that the Holy Spirit gives not only spiritual gifts to the believer, but also joy, peace and hope. We don't have to go through life remaining fearful. Through the Holy Spirit, God gives us the power to perform anything that He has asked us to do—including being loving parents to the little ones He gives us. 🐾

$\mathcal{B}$ehold, the eye of the LORD is
on those who fear Him,
On those who hope in His
mercy.

Psalm 33:18

A New Road

Psalm 33:18

Barb fumbled with the words as she told me of her pattern of involvement with alcoholics—two former husbands and a current boyfriend.

"But what can I expect?" she asked. "I wasn't the best teenager in the world. God's giving me what I deserve. I just don't want Him punishing my kids too."

God wasn't punishing her or her children. She was punishing herself. For the next hour, we talked about her destructive choices. As she remembers the decisions she's made, she will see that God has also provided a way out. As she gives herself permission to choose new patterns, she will start seeing His blessings and the ways He can help as she looks to Him.

Any relationship with God must start with seeing the love that sent His Son to die on the Cross. From there we must trust that He is with us, helping us make decisions. As we fear Him, in a respectful and thankful way, He offers us better choices.

The unbeliever has every reason to panic at thoughts of God, for he stands condemned before Him. This kind of fear can lead to repentance, or to a feeble attempt to hide from God or even deny His existence. But His mercy and His boundless compassion extend to all who will receive His gifts. And as our loving heavenly Father, He can meet the needs of those who ask for His help. 🙢

$\mathcal{A}$bove all, taking the shield of faith with which you will be able to quench all the fiery darts of the wicked one.

Apostle Paul
Ephesians 6:16

God's Strong Armor
Ephesians 6:16

Nickie felt as though she was being hit from all sides. She didn't fit in at school, she had flunked math for the second time, she wasn't getting along with her dad, her boyfriend dumped her because she was pregnant, and she knew if she told her parents, they'd probably kick her out of the house.

If that wasn't enough, her older sister told her, "I envy you. You don't have bills to pay or any responsibilities. You better enjoy this. These are the best years of your life." Nickie shivered. If *these* were the best years, what awful things were waiting in the future?

In Ephesians, Paul describes a scene Nickie could identify with: the bombardment in war. During ancient times, arrows were covered with tar, set afire and shot into the enemy lines. The advancing soldiers used their shields to ward off the "fiery darts."

Most of us have times when we feel as though we are under bombardment. Our warfare is not against physical armies, but against invisible evil powers. The only way to protect ourselves is to wear God's promises and take a battle stance against this unseen satanic structure. Our faith, our dependence on and confidence in God, is our shield which can protect us against Satan's most fiery attacks.

$\mathcal{T}$ake heed that you do not despise one of these little ones, for I say to you that in heaven their angels always see the face of My Father who is in heaven.

Jesus
Matthew 18:10

In Our Hands

Matthew 18:10

Caught in a taxi in the middle of downtown traffic, I could only relax. I gawked at the tall buildings and marveled at the various nationalities of people swarming the sidewalks. As we inched forward, I noticed a little girl standing alone. People were rushing by, ignoring the obviously fearful child. My thoughts bumped against one another: *That's somebody's little girl. How can people ignore her? Lord, protect her. I'll take her to the police station.*

Just as I leaned forward to tell the driver I'd get out, a frantic woman darted around the corner, spotted the child and ran to her, calling her name. When the mother swooped her up, both sobbed at having found one another.

I said a "Thank You, Lord" and settled back, also thankful He had allowed me to see the rescue. But I was also sad as I thought of the countless situations with unhappy endings. If my pain as a human is that great, then how much more our perfect heavenly Father's pain must be.

God has promised to rescue anyone who calls Him, but He also has left many things to us. One of those responsibilities is caring for children, whether they're born or pre-born. These little ones are so important to Him that Jesus told His disciples their angels behold God's face. That should make them even more important to us too. ❧

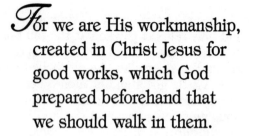

$\mathcal{F}$or we are His workmanship,
created in Christ Jesus for
good works, which God
prepared beforehand that
we should walk in them.

Apostle Paul
Ephesians 2:10

God's Handiwork

Ephesians 2:10

In my old cedar chest is the baby quilt I made for Holly years ago. Even with repeated washing, the embroidered threads creating the blue elephants and pink flowers are still bright—and still show the love stitched into the fabric.

In this Ephesians verse of Scripture, Paul is comparing believers to God's workmanship as he uses the Greek word *poiema,* which means "to make" and is the source of our English word "poem." Since the word describes products from talented artisans, we have the image that we are works of art, His poems.

Truly, a born-again believer is a masterpiece of God. And as I think of the raw materials, especially my feisty personality, He has to work with, His achievement is all the more remarkable. I'm convinced God has a blueprint for each of us and that He begins to unfold it when we realize that Jesus died on the Cross for us. We can spare ourselves the frenzy of trying to run our own lives by believing in Jesus. God gives us the Bible and other Christians to help us turn our lives over to Him. Then we'll find that we truly are His work of art and we can become the parents He wants us to be.

Cast all your care upon Him, for
He cares for you.

Apostle Peter
1 Peter 5:7

Our Father's Care

1 Peter 5:7

A father called, "Daddy's got ya," as he swooped up a laughing toddler trying to outrun him in the mall. The child giggled and then snuggled against his neck.

Suddenly I remembered a long-ago night in our Kentucky farm community. I was five years old, and my parents had taken me down the road to visit neighbors. By the time we left, the stars were out, and our lane looked long and dark in the moonlight, especially where the thornbushes hung over the ditches. Quickly, my dad swooped me up and carried me on his strong shoulders. I felt so safe and warm that I fell asleep.

That's the way it is for all of us who are children of our heavenly Father. Notice that the verse in 1 Peter doesn't promise we won't have problems, just that when they come, we can confidently give them to Him through prayer.

The word "care" is used in two ways here—our worry and His comfort. The worrying type of care comes from the word *meiro,* which means "to divide the mind." Thus, the word suggests worries, distractions and anxieties. Those burdens are unnecessary though, because the Father's love provides for both our daily needs and our special needs. Besides, worrying doesn't solve problems; it actually creates more.

So let's cast our anxieties on the Lord with the confidence that no matter what problems we see "down the road," we can rest on His heavenly shoulders and let Him carry us past life's thornbushes and ditches.

$\mathcal{T}$hen God said, "Let Us make man in Our image, according to Our likeness; let them have dominion over the fish of the sea, over the birds of the air, and over the cattle, over all the earth and over every creeping thing that creeps on the earth."

Genesis 1:26

In God's Image

Genesis 1:26

Our son, Jay, was born one bright October morning. As I heard him yell in protest at being thrust from his warm, dark sanctuary into a cold, yellow room, the doctor said, "You have a son. And he's perfect."

But *hearing* of his perfection couldn't compare to that moment when the nurse handed him to me. I looked at him in awe, whispered, "Hello, sweetheart," and kissed his tiny hands.

Isn't being created in God's image an incredible idea? As God speaks in Genesis, He was talking not only to the rest of the Trinity (the Son and the Holy Spirit) but to the angels—the entire host of heaven—as well. Only the Son would later have an earthly body, so the "image" spoken of here undoubtedly refers to the human's ability to think, hear, see and speak. To be created in the image of God also means that we have His love and the ability and privilege of knowing and loving Him.

Very soon after God made man, He gave him authority over the earth. Notice He says, "let *them* have dominion." He planned from the beginning that Adam and Eve would populate the earth. If we remember that every human life is precious to God, we will treat carefully the people with whom we share the world.

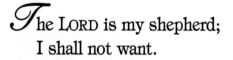

The LORD is my shepherd;
  I shall not want.

David
Psalm 23:1

Part of His Flock

Psalm 23:1

The young woman who came through the door of the crisis pregnancy center couldn't have been more than twenty. She was tall and slim with shining black hair. In a whisper, she asked the receptionist if she could get a pregnancy test. As she waited to be called into the counselor's office, she twisted and untwisted her purse straps. Her attention darted to the plants, the magazines and the colorful window blinds. Then she looked at the black-and-white drawing near the door of Jesus nuzzling a lamb and visibly relaxed. She'd just been reminded she wasn't alone.

The Twenty-third Psalm is one of the most familiar passages in the Old Testament. Written by David, the king who had once tended his father's flocks on lonely hillsides, it gives a picture of the Lord as the Good Shepherd, protecting and providing for His sheep. The first verse summarizes the entire passage: with Him as our Shepherd, we have it all.

Imagine a shepherd who watches over his flock, takes them to the good water and meadows, protects and guides them, invites them to a banquet where they are well protected, even within sight of their enemies, provides the goodness and mercy so desperately needed in this life, and promises a secure and eternal dwelling place. That's quite a picture!

Jesus as the Good Shepherd went one step beyond David's list of provisions—He gave His life for His sheep. And because of His sacrifice we can dwell with Him forever, not as a guest but part of His family. There's no safer place than in His flock.

$\mathcal{B}$e anxious for nothing, but in everything by prayer and supplication, with thanksgiving, let your requests be made known to God; and the peace of God, which surpasses all understanding, will guard your hearts and minds through Christ Jesus.

Apostle Paul
Philippians 4:6-7

Heart-filling Peace
Philippians 4:6-7

When we brought Jay home from the hospital, I hovered near his crib, to be sure he was breathing normally. If he coughed, I worried. If he hiccupped, I worried. But by the time Holly arrived sixteen and a half months later, it finally had occurred to me that worry didn't do anything but make me lose sleep. As I learned to relax a little and pray a lot, I enjoyed both children more.

The word "anxious" that Paul uses in his letter to the church in Philippi comes from *merimnaō*, which means "to be distracted." And isn't that what worry is? Something to distract us and keep our attention on the problem rather than on the solution? Paul's remedy for worry is to pray about everything and then anticipate God's loving reply just as He has answered past problems.

Is it really possible to "be anxious for nothing"? Let this former worrier assure you that it is—as long as we keep praying. Worrying makes us doubt God's ability to help. Once we learn to take *everything* to Him in prayer, His peace fills our days. Everything means everything. Nothing is too great or too small to talk over with Him!

Prayer is both an action and an attitude as we learn to leave things in His hands. "Supplication" suggests intense, extended prayer as we transfer our burden into God's hands. But it is only as we give God our worrisome situations—whether we're hovering over cribs or pacing the floor on date night—that we will escape the nagging, paralyzing anxiety and experience His peace. 🎜

$\mathcal{B}$lessed is the man who endures temptation; for when he has been approved, he will receive the crown of life which the Lord has promised to those who love Him.

James the Just
James 1:12

Ultimate Victory

James 1:12

Whenever I'd complain to Mama Farley about what I considered another trial in my young life, she'd look at me sympathetically and say, "Honey, there are some things in life that all you can do with 'em is bear 'em. Just keep looking to the Lord; He'll get you through." Of course, I didn't feel like bearing my problems; I wanted them removed.

How do we normally react when tragedy, disappointment or even temptation comes into our lives? Do we complain bitterly about the rotten deal, or do we thank the Lord for being with us in the midst of trouble? Do we live only in the future, waiting for our lot to improve, or do we live today, looking for evidence of God's presence? Do we indulge in daily "pity parties," or do we look for ways to lessen our pain by helping others?

In the verse from James, he concludes his discussion of trials with a blessing on those who withstand afflictions. When we have come through the experience, we will receive the crown of life. The crown here is not a jeweled diadem, but a victor's wreath presented to long distance runners. And we don't have to wait until heaven to receive it; our daily lives can be blessed as we enjoy life more fully because of having endured.

Mama Farley was right: how much better to bear our trials with the Lord's help. And it begins with asking for His help.

Call upon Me in the day of
    trouble;
I will deliver you, and you
    shall glorify Me.

Psalm 50:15

God's Way Out

Psalm 50:15

When Holly was a toddler, her favorite expression was "Me do!" It didn't matter if she wanted to pour her own cereal, get dressed or tie her shoes; she had to be in charge. Of course I should have been glad she was determined to be independent, but she wasn't old enough to have fine tuned the needed skills. She'd spill the cereal—hardly my favorite sight when we were in a hurry—put her shirt on backward and get her laces so knotted that I'd have to work a fork prong through the knots to untie them one by one.

Sadly, don't we do the same thing to the Lord? He gives us clear instructions about life, leading us step by step and helping us make good decisions, when we'll let Him. But, no, we get our moral laces all in knots.

I'll say this for Holly, though. When she'd gotten her shoe laces hopelessly tangled, she'd hand me the shoe and say, "You do." Then she'd watch as I'd untie them.

That's what God has promised us: "Give Me the knotted laces of your life. No matter what you've done to get yourself into this mess, I'll help you, if you'll let Me. Then you'll see My power, praise Me and tell others about Me."

Notice that He doesn't promise we won't have trouble in this life, just that He will rescue us. Doesn't that sound like a good reason to turn to Him and say, "You do!"

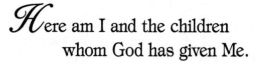

*H*ere am I and the children
whom God has given Me.

Hebrews 2:13b

A Precious Gift

Hebrews 2:13b

The couple kept pacing near Gate 7 as they waited for a plane from Seattle. Occasionally the young woman would look at her husband for reassurance. He'd put his arm around her, kiss her forehead, and the pacing would begin again. At last the plane touched down and began taxiing to the gate. The young couple embraced as they watched the door. The young woman was trembling.

An airport representative approached, saying, "She'll be the last one off. A stewardess will bring her." Then she hugged the woman, and added, "Don't worry. You guys will be great parents."

Parents! They were waiting for the child they were going to adopt. By now everyone's attention was directed to the door, and most of us were crying too. We watched every passenger get off. Then finally a stewardess came up the hallway carrying a dark-haired little girl about a year old. Gently, she handed the blinking child to her delighted parents.

Children. Life does not contain anything more precious than the life of a little one—whether that child is born to us or comes through adoption.

In Hebrews 2, we are reminded of Christ's life on earth, as He took human form to identify with our struggles and willingly became the sacrifice for our sins. The words from this verse are also found in Isaiah 8:18 where the thought is we are members of a common family, acknowledging a common Father. I can't imagine anything more profound than presenting our children to our heavenly Father, not only here on earth but in heaven. How wonderful to be able to say when we someday stand before almighty God, "Here am I and the children whom You gave to me."

$\mathcal{B}$eing confident of this very
thing, that He who has begun
a good work in you will com-
plete it until the day of Jesus
Christ.

Apostle Paul
Philippians 1:6

Nothing Unfinished

Philippians 1:6

Before Cathy's son was born, she bought four yards of calico to make a baby quilt like one in a woman's magazine. For several evenings she cut the little squares and then stitched half of the pattern. Soon, though, she tired of it and put it aside for later. The baby arrived the next month, and Cathy never got back to the quilt. It's still in a guest room bottom drawer, where it's been for seventeen years.

Aren't we glad God doesn't start projects and then abandon them? In Philippians 1:6, the Apostle Paul states that his confidence in the Philippians' ability to remain spiritually strong until Jesus returns is based not on their power but on God's— and on His ability to perform in them a good work. The word "good" is used in both a physical and moral sense of something that produces an excellent product in people or situations.

Sometimes, however, we panic because we can't see what God is doing, or we think He isn't doing at all. When I have those moments, I dwell on a quotation from Dwight L. Moody, the great nineteenth-century evangelist and founder of Moody Bible Institute: "Don't doubt in the dark what God has shown you in the light." In other words, don't let worry and unresolved situations wear down your faith and trust in the things God can reveal. He will do what He says, and He will finish what He has started. ❧

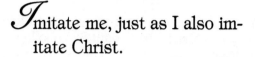

*I*mitate me, just as I also imitate Christ.

Apostle Paul
1 Corinthians 11:1

Setting a Good Example

1 Corinthians 11:1

Curt returned to the office late one evening, bringing his three-year-old son along. From my desk, I could see down the long, dark corridor, but Curt couldn't see me.

The child kept glancing up adoringly as he tried to copy his dad's big steps. Curt grabbed a chair as he leaned across his desk to look for a forgotten item. The child put his hand against another chair in the same way.

At last, Curt found the needed papers and called a cheery, "Okay, son, let's go." As they headed toward the elevator, Curt started singing "Jesus Loves Me." The little boy grinned and then added his timid soprano to his father's baritone.

Suddenly the corridor wasn't quite as dark as it had been.

Like it or not, people watch us as we go about even the most ordinary chores each day. Not only do our children watch us, but they imitate us. Obviously, it's vitally important that we are aware of the example we set.

Before the 1 Corinthians 11 verse, Paul had told his followers in the city of Corinth how he tried to choose his actions according to the effect they would have on others. He reminded them how he tried to help those about him by being unselfish and living a simple life-style, like Jesus. He also knew that "imitate" requires continuous action, not a one-shot deal. And the best way to be the example we need to be is by imitating the Lord—the One who can give us guidance as we guide our children. 🐚

*Y*ou are of God, little children,
and have overcome them,
because He who is in you
is greater than he who is
in the world.

Apostle John
1 John 4:4

God's Greater Strength

1 John 4:4

Don and I married while we were in college. A year later, just before my graduation, we thought about starting our family. At the same time, a radical group took over the campus. Every evening the police arrested another batch of angry students who had tossed smoke bombs through classroom windows. Suddenly this activity was more than a political disagreement; it represented everything that could threaten our future children.

One Sunday afternoon, I blurted all this to my mother. She listened and then handed me a tissue. "I remember being afraid too," she said. "It was wartime when your dad and I worried about having you. But the Lord brought us through a tough time. He'll take you through this too."

I'm glad I listened to her; I would have missed incredible blessings if I had let fear control my future.

When we start to worry, we have to concentrate on the Lord's power instead of Satan's destructive forces. God is greater than the Enemy, and no matter what comes our way, He will be with us just as He has been with other parents throughout troubling times.

When those fearful thoughts come, we need to take a deep breath and remind ourselves that the God who loved us enough to send His only Son to save us from our sins *is* with us and that He is stronger than anything the world or the Enemy can throw our way. 🍃

$\mathcal{A}$nd my God shall supply all your need according to His riches in glory by Christ Jesus.

Apostle Paul
Philippians 4:19

God's Provision

Philippians 4:19

"But I can't have a baby *now!*" Have you ever thought that? Most women have at one time or another. But it's like my mother says, "If you wait until the 'right' time to have a baby, you'll never have one."

Marcy was single and working to put herself through college when she became pregnant. Abortion was her first thought.

Jerry and Pat were in graduate school when they found out they would be parents. They needed Pat's job; now she would have to quit. This was not a good time to have a baby.

But instead of abortion, the three young parents gulped and decided to give life. Marcy placed her son in a two-parent family and continued with her education. The ache of wondering what he's like will always stay with her, but at least she knows he's with parents who desperately wanted a child. She doesn't have to cringe when she hears about the garbage bags from abortion clinics.

Jerry and Pat found that their budget and schedule gradually stretched to include the little boy who looks like his daddy. Now, they can't imagine their lives without him.

When we start to panic and think that whatever situation we're facing is impossible, we need to think of Paul's message to the Philippian church. Whatever need we have, God can fill. Notice that He doesn't promise to supply all our *wants*, but all we need. Come to think of it, that's a tall order— and a wonderful promise. 🍃

$\mathcal{F}$inally, brethren, whatever
things are true, whatever
things are noble, what-
ever things are just, whatever
things are pure, whatever
things are lovely, whatever
things are of good report, if
there is any virtue and if there
is anything praiseworthy—
meditate on these things.

Apostle Paul
Philippians 4:8

A Wise Choice

Philippians 4:8

Carol was difficult to be around. Even when she learned she was pregnant, after months of trying, she wouldn't allow herself to get excited. If someone congratulated her, she merely nodded and turned away. Even after their healthy boy was born, she maintained her gloom-and-doom attitude.

Her husband finally became concerned, and rightly so, that her attitude would affect their child, and he insisted she counsel with their pastor. In the first session, the pastor asked her to memorize Philippians 4:8 and bring examples of "good report" each week. At first, the assignments were difficult because she wasn't used to thinking in such terms. But as she forced herself to look for blessings, she found them more readily. Anyone meeting her today wouldn't believe she is the same person.

In the highlighted verse, the Apostle Paul is encouraging believers in Philippi to choose well. "Good report" comes from the word *euphemos,* which means speech that is gracious, kind and full of honest praise. This passage deals with our thought life too. When we have a wicked thought, we should immediately get rid of it by meditating on the Person and work of Christ we can know through the Bible, prayer and being with other believers. Because of His power, we *can* choose well.

Admittedly, we all have times when we're convinced nothing will work out, but dwelling on the possible pain robs us of the joy. We do have choices how we will respond to the crises in our lives. We can withdraw from life, or we can choose to let God bring His good out of all that is happening. It's up to us. ❧

$\mathcal{T}$hen they brought little children to Him, that He might touch them; but the disciples rebuked those who brought them. But when Jesus saw it, He was greatly displeased and said to them, "Let the little children come to Me, and do not forbid them; for of such is the kingdom of God. Assuredly, I say to you, whoever does not receive the kingdom of God as a little child will by no means enter it." And He took them up in His arms, laid His hands on them, and blessed them.

Mark 10:13-16

Blessing Our Children

Mark 10:13-16

I wanted to get my daughter, Holly, from the church nursery, but one of my grumpy colleagues kept asking me questions about our new teachers' contract. Marilyn, the nursery worker, saw us, and she opened the gate so Holly could run to me.

As I swooped up my little girl, the man frowned and turned to talk to another teacher. I pushed my face against Holly's sweet-smelling neck, rejoicing that she was more important than any argument.

In the passage from Mark, religious leaders had been arguing with Jesus about picky points of the Law. When He and His disciples are alone again, they ask Him to clarify His thoughts about divorce. In the midst of the discussion, parents show up with their families, wanting Jesus to bless the children. The disciples, convinced the Master has more important things to do, try to send the people away. But Jesus sees the little ones and insists that the disciples let the children come to Him, explaining that God's kingdom belongs to those who have childlike faith and humility.

This account is a touching reminder that Jesus is concerned for all who are helpless and see their need for Him.

$\mathscr{P}$eace I leave with you, My
peace I give to you; not as the
world gives do I give to you.
Let not your heart be troubled,
neither let it be afraid.

Jesus
John 14:27

Unending Peace
John 14:27

What's the most frightening thing you've ever faced? For some of us it was the illness of our child or the loss of a job. But for one of my high school students, Debbie, it was having to tell her parents that she was pregnant. Determined to have an abortion, she talked with a school counselor. Remembering the other girls he'd had to counsel *after* their abortions, he asked her to think about it a little more. He even suggested she tell a trusted relative first, to gauge the reaction. Debbie chose to confide in her favorite aunt, who promptly offered to stand by her no matter what the parents said. Suddenly the future looked a little brighter.

Debbie learned it is possible to have peace in the midst of turmoil. In fact, often when we acknowledge that we have an impossible situation, then we are forced to acknowledge that only God can help.

Jesus' words in John 14 tell of promised peace. As He and His disciples ate their last meal together, He gave His last will and testament. But He didn't leave material things. Instead He left the inner peace that comes when we allow Him to give us a new life. His gift of peace is forever. It is a mixture of hope, trust and calm that says we don't have to be afraid—no matter what situations we face. ❧

Pregnancy Record

The
Pre-birth Story
of:

_____

from _____

to _____

(baby's birth date)

Recorded by:

_____

(baby's mother)

Life Anew

Hints of Life *(pregnancy symptoms)* _____

_____

_____

_____

Thoughts _____

_____

_____

_____

_____

_____

_____

_____

_____

_____

_____

_____

Favorite Names _____

_____

_____

_____

The First Doctor's Visit

Name _____ Date _____

Address _____ Phone _____

Height _____ Weight _____

Blood Pressure _____ Blood Type & RH _____

Doctor's Advice _____

_____

_____

_____

_____

_____

_____

_____

_____

_____

Record of Family Illnesses _____

_____

_____

_____

Month 1

Thoughts _____
_____
_____
_____
_____
_____
_____

Best Memory Made _____
_____
_____
_____

Doctor's Advice _____
_____
_____
_____

This Month's To-Do List _____
_____
_____
_____
_____
_____

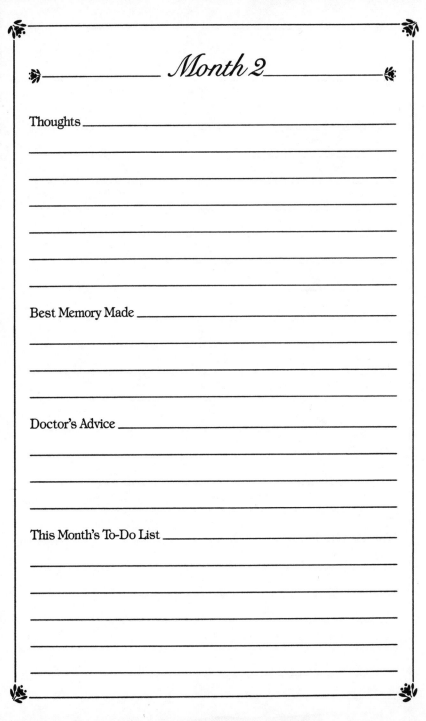

Month 2

Thoughts _____

_____

_____

_____

_____

_____

_____

Best Memory Made _____

_____

_____

_____

Doctor's Advice _____

_____

_____

_____

This Month's To-Do List _____

_____

_____

_____

_____

_____

Month 3

Thoughts _____
_____
_____
_____
_____
_____
_____

Best Memory Made _____
_____
_____
_____

Doctor's Advice _____
_____
_____
_____

This Month's To-Do List _____
_____
_____
_____
_____
_____

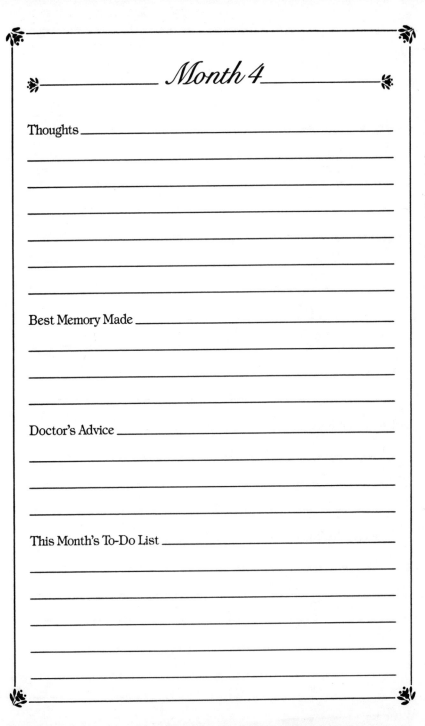

Month 4

Thoughts _____

_____

_____

_____

_____

_____

_____

Best Memory Made _____

_____

_____

_____

Doctor's Advice _____

_____

_____

_____

This Month's To-Do List _____

_____

_____

_____

_____

_____

Month 5

Thoughts _____
_____
_____
_____
_____
_____
_____

Best Memory Made _____
_____
_____
_____

Doctor's Advice _____
_____
_____
_____

This Month's To-Do List _____
_____
_____
_____
_____
_____

Month 6

Thoughts _____
_____
_____
_____
_____
_____
_____

Best Memory Made _____
_____
_____
_____

Doctor's Advice _____
_____
_____
_____

This Month's To-Do List _____
_____
_____
_____
_____
_____

Month 7

Thoughts _____

_____

_____

_____

_____

_____

_____

Best Memory Made _____

_____

_____

_____

Doctor's Advice _____

_____

_____

_____

This Month's To-Do List _____

_____

_____

_____

_____

_____

Month 8

Thoughts _____

_____

_____

_____

_____

_____

_____

Best Memory Made _____

_____

_____

_____

Doctor's Advice _____

_____

_____

_____

This Month's To-Do List _____

_____

_____

_____

_____

_____

Month 9

Thoughts _____
_____
_____
_____
_____
_____
_____

Best Memory Made _____
_____
_____
_____

Doctor's Advice _____
_____
_____
_____

This Month's To-Do List _____
_____
_____
_____
_____
_____

Baby Will Need

- ☐ Diapers
  (cloth or disposable)
- ☐ Diaper pins
- ☐ Plastic or rubber pants
- ☐ Sleepers
- ☐ Socks, booties
- ☐ Undershirts
- ☐ Bibs
- ☐ Sweater, bonnet
- ☐ Receiving blankets
- ☐ Crib, cradle or bassinet
- ☐ Mattress
- ☐ Crib bumper

- ☐ Crib sheets
- ☐ Waterproof pads
- ☐ Crib blanket
- ☐ Dresser
- ☐ Diaper pail, covered
- ☐ Baby bathtub
- ☐ Rectal thermometer
- ☐ Disposable wipes
- ☐ Baby washcloths
- ☐ Changing table

Other
- ☐ Sterilized bottles, nipples
- ☐ Pads, bras

- ☐ Cotton balls
- ☐ Approved infant car seat
- ☐ Small baby carrier
- ☐ Stroller
- ☐ Comb, brush set
- ☐ Diaper bag
- ☐ Night light
- ☐ Laundry hamper
- ☐ Bottle and nipple brushes
- ☐ High chair
- ☐ Baby album

For Hospital Stay

- ☐ Preadmission forms
- ☐ Toiletry articles
  (toothbrush, deodorant, shampoo, etc.)
- ☐ Cosmetics, curlers
- ☐ Nightgowns *(at least two)*
- ☐ Bathrobe
- ☐ Slippers
- ☐ Nursing/support bra
- ☐ Going home outfit
  (Remember you will still look about four months pregnant.) Include underwear

- ☐ Baby's going home outfit
  (diapers, shirt, pins, sweater, hat, blanket)
- ☐ Watch
- ☐ Insurance papers
- ☐ Sock with two tennis balls in it *(use for back massage or pressure to lower back during contractions)*
- ☐ Chapstick *(lips get dry during labor)*
- ☐ Camera
- ☐ Hairbrush and pins or bands to keep hair out of face

- ☐ Change for vending machines
- ☐ Handicraft, games or books
- ☐ Pregnancy Record *(don't forget to update after delivery)*

Emergency Numbers

Taxi: _____

Ambulance: _____

Baby-sitter: _____

Grandma: _____

Hospital: _____

Doctor/midwife: _____

Police: _____

Fire: _____

Other: _____

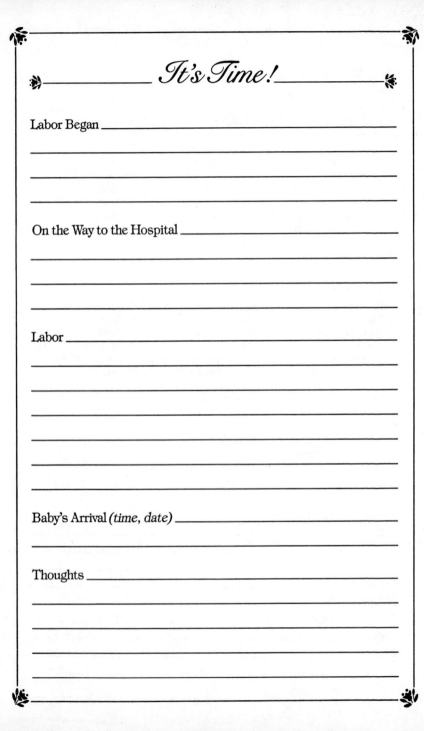

It's Time!

Labor Began _____

_____

_____

_____

On the Way to the Hospital _____

_____

_____

_____

Labor _____

_____

_____

_____

_____

_____

_____

Baby's Arrival *(time, date)* _____

_____

Thoughts _____

_____

_____

_____

_____